clean your home healthy

green cleaning made easy

Candita Clayton
with Bryna René

New York

clean your home healthy
green cleaning made easy

ISBN: 978-1-60037-409-8 (Paperback)
Library of Congress Number: 2008921257

Published by:

www.morganjamespublishing.com

Habitat for Humanity®
Peninsula Building Partner

Morgan James Publishing, LLC
1225 Franklin Ave. Ste 325
Garden City, NY 11530-1693
Toll Free 800-485-4943
www.MorganJamesPublishing.com

Cover/Interior Design by:
Marianna Zotos
marizot@gmail.com

for Tom, who makes all things possible

inside

your
life
organized

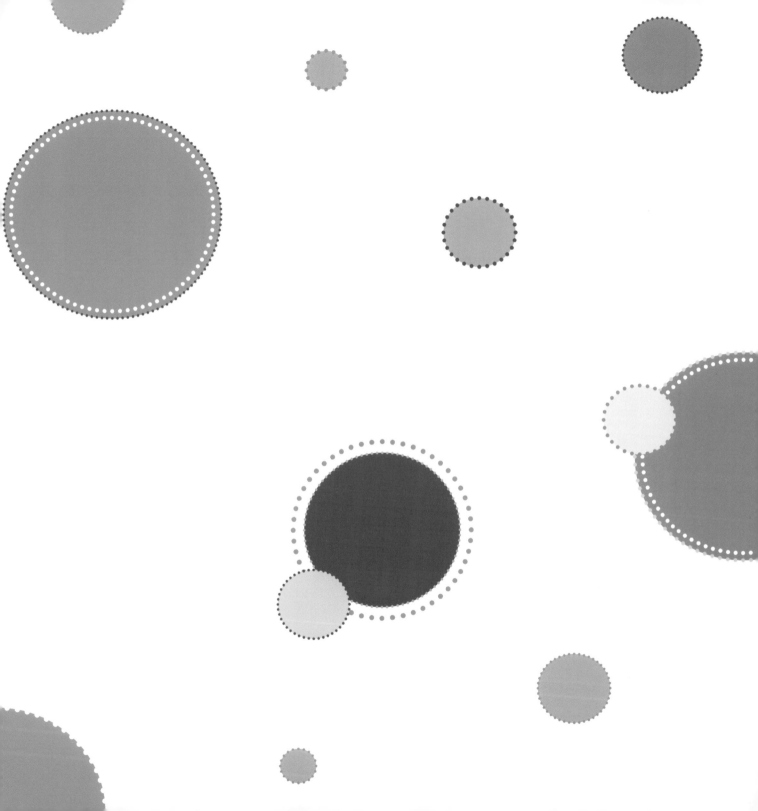

your life...organized

In my career as a professional home organizer, I have discovered time and time again that an organized living space can reduce stress, minimize cleaning time, and help every daily routine run smoothly. Study after study has proven that less stress leads to better health, so I think it's fair to say that an organized home is a healthier home, hands down.

But to truly clean your home healthy, it's necessary to move beyond organizing. Many factors which dramatically impact the health of a home have little or nothing to do with a well-laid-out closet or a tidy pantry. For example, the EPA estimates that household air can be 2 to 10 times more polluted than outdoor air. Some studies cite levels of pollution at 70 times higher than outdoor air. While most of us have heard some variant of that statistic before, we brush it off, telling ourselves that those numbers apply only to smokers, crazy cat ladies, and people who never dust. Unfortunately, that's not the way it works.

There are many factors which can influence the level of pollution inside a home, including smoking and the ubiquitous pet dander, as well as specific building materials used in a home, the home's age, and the presence of mold or mildew.
But what may surprise you is that some of the biggest spoilers of indoor air quality are the household cleaning products we use every day. Not only do many common cleaning products have a significant impact on our health, they also wreak havoc on our planet once they're rinsed down the drain. When you consider the number of chemical compounds we spray, spritz, squirt, and pour around our homes every week, exposure times add up quick. The good news is, these pollutants are among the easiest to get rid of... all you have to do is go non-toxic!

I wrote *Clean Your Home Healthy: Green Cleaning Made Easy* to help people make educated decisions about the cleaning products they use in their homes. The suggestions are easy to implement, and the products suggested usually cost about the same as the commercial stuff – less, in some cases. When we, as consumers, support eco-conscious companies who use naturally derived ingredients and safe manufacturing practices, we're also helping to create a healthier environment for our families and a healthier planet for everyone.

Now don't panic: you don't have to radically change your life to improve the quality of your home environment. Going green doesn't have to involve moving to the arctic wilderness or trading your work shoes for Birkenstocks. In fact, you probably won't even have to alter your core routine: there are hundreds of great non-toxic and environmentally conscious products on the market today, and with the green trend on the rise, even big-box retailers are starting to take notice. If your local supermarket isn't carrying what you need, you can always shop online – and save gas in the bargain. And don't underestimate the power of small changes, like exchanging light bulbs or buying recycled toilet paper: these things do make a difference, not only in the future, but right now.

As you begin to take the first steps towards 'greening' your home, you may encounter some skepticism. Your spouse may not understand why you have stopped using their favorite dryer sheets, or why natural products are so important. Your mother-in-law may insist that the only way to get a floor clean is by bleaching it. Today's kids, growing up in a world where everything is disposable, may find it hard to adjust to the idea of not just tossing everything into the trash, or using recycled paper products. I don't say this to discourage, but rather to encourage you to prepare yourself for the opinions you may encounter, and to urge you to maintain your commitment to providing the safest, healthiest home environment for your family. From my own experience, I believe you'll see a difference in the way you feel almost immediately, especially if you or someone in your household suffers from respiratory ailments like asthma, or from chronic allergies.

Don't worry if you can't use all of the suggestions in this book right away. Remember that change is a process: neither you, nor those around you, can expect to wake up tomorrow and instantly change lifelong habits. Set manageable goals and learn what works for you and what doesn't. You are moving toward a lifetime of better health, and as you go you will continue to evaluate and evolve your practices. As you learn more and more about the benefits of ridding your home of toxic products, changes that seemed impractical will suddenly feel natural. Take advantage of the opportunity to teach your kids what you learn and help them understand that the actions you (and they) take today are meant to improve the world that they will one day be responsible for. And please, share your challenges and successes with me - it's always so wonderful to hear from others who are committed to healthy living and a healthy planet.

One more thing: Although I have done a lot of research - including testing the recommendations in my own home – I'm not a doctor or an environmental scientist. That's why I've left most of the technical talk out, focusing instead on essential information that you need to know right away. Rather than fill hundreds of pages with studies and statistics, I've included a comprehensive list of resources at the end of this book, so you can look over those studies and stats for yourself, and share what you learn with those you care about.

room by room

Most calls to the national Poison Control Center are initiated because of ingestion, inhalation or exposure to everyday household chemicals. The most common culprit? Chlorine bleach (a.k.a. sodium hypochlorite), which is present in everything from automatic dishwashing detergents to laundry preparations to toilet bowl cleaners. In fact, bleach is to blame for nearly 40% of all household poisonings in the U.S. each year[1].

Also high on the toxic countdown is ammonia, which can also be found in any number of commercial household products, including floor cleaners and glass cleaners[1]. Ammonia can burn skin and eyes, is highly dangerous if ingested, and can aggravate respiratory conditions like asthma and bronchitis.

You don't need to douse your home in toxic chemicals to keep it spic and span. In fact, if there's a surface to be cleaned, chances are there's a natural and non-toxic product to clean it with. Transitioning to a green cleaning routine is simple: when you run out of your current product, simply replace it with its natural, non-toxic counterpart. It's that easy.

In the following chapters, I'll take you through each room in your house and address cleaning issues common to each area. In the 'Back to Basics' section I'll share some of my favorite tips on how to use the Fab Five — hydrogen peroxide, lemon juice, white vinegar, castile soap, and baking soda. The Non-toxic Nurseries section explains how you can create a clean, healthy environment for your little one through conscientious cleaning, decorating, and renovation.

I hope that these chapters will not only introduce you to great companies and resources, but help you understand why it's so important to clean your home healthy.

I've said it before, and I'll say it again: even small changes can make a big difference. So read on, and go green!

bedroom bliss

You probably spend more time in your bedroom than in any other room in your house. In fact, if you sleep eight hours a night, you'll spend a third of your life in bed – and a third of your life exposed to whatever chemicals you're using in your bedroom. But don't lose sleep over it: a few simple changes can transform your boudoir into a healthy, eco-friendly retreat. Now won't that help you sleep more soundly?

What are you washing your jammies in? Chlorine bleach and the petroleum-based surfactants found in many laundry detergents can be irritating to your respiratory tract and skin. Reducing your exposure to these chemicals is a positive step toward a more restful night's sleep. Try **Seventh Generation's** Free and Clear laundry powder (seventhgeneration.com).

Change your sheets! Organic cotton sheets, blankets and duvets are easier to find than ever before, and they're surprisingly affordable, especially if you opt for cotton jersey or flannel varieties.

Why go organic? For starters, traditionally processed cotton is full of pesticide residues and is bleached with chlorine before it's dyed; this process creates VOC's (Volatile Organic Compounds, some of the most poisonous chemicals known to man), which are released into our groundwater and soil. Synthetic fabrics like polyester are made entirely from chemicals – and, like their close relative plastic, they require lots of petroleum to produce. Also, fabrics that have been treated to prevent wrinkles may contain formaldehyde[2,3]. All these chemicals make toxic bedfellows – and they don't come off in a single washing. Also good to know: purchasing organically grown cotton supports free trade and sustainable farming practices.

If you're sensitive or allergy-prone, or if you're interested in upgrading, consider pillows filled with natural fiber fill, feather or down. Down has a bad rap as a real allergy trigger, but studies show that synthetic pillows and bedding attract 10 times more dust mites than their feather and down counterparts – and as anyone with indoor allergies knows, those little buggers aren't pleasant to have around[4]. Also, natural fiber pillow cases with a high thread count help to keep dust mites out. Check out theorganicmattressstore.com, and see Resources for a full list of retailers.

studies show that synthetic pillows and bedding attract 10 times more dust mites than their feather and down counterparts

bedroom bliss

Put a little Zen in your den. Try burning subtle cedar or sandalwood incense blends. Another upside to incense – cool burners, which double as decor.

When you're setting the mood for love, make sure you're lighting natural soy candles. Paraffin wax, which most candles are made of, is a petroleum derivative that emits 11 known toxins when burned[5]. Also, many scented candles use chemical fragrances that can be severely irritating to your respiratory tract, and there's nothing romantic about that. See Resources for a list of retailers and how to learn more.

Give your bedroom the attention it deserves when it comes to cleaning. Change bed linens once a week. Dust with a microfiber cloth and a little warm water, or with a magnetic duster. Don't use commercial dusting sprays, as these contain chemical fragrances, petroleum-based surfactants and shine enhancers, none of which are good to breathe. Weekly vacuuming will also improve air quality and keep your sanctuary clean and welcoming.

Coats and shoes worn day in and day out may absorb pollutants and chemical residues – like those from lawn and garden pesticides, cigarette smoke, even your workplace. Consider leaving your shoes at the door when you come home: wipe them down before returning them to your bedroom closet. For overcoats and other outdoor gear, an airy mudroom or entry closet is a much better home than your bedroom closet. All coats should be washed or cleaned by an eco-friendly dry cleaner before they're stored for the summer.

> **WANT TO LEARN MORE?**
> Find out what's really in your current products by visiting the household products database at www.hpd.nlm.nih.gov/.
>
> You can also check out Seventh Generation's chemical glossary: visit www.seventhgeneration.com and click on Home Safety.

Dry Clean Only? While your newly dry cleaned clothes may look fresh and clean, they could be polluting the air in your closet, your bedroom, and your entire house. If you must dry clean, remove your clothes from the plastic bags and let them air out on your porch or in your garage before bringing them inside.

For more on dry cleaning, check out section 5: ... and don't forget your laundry.

bedroom bliss

Easy Care? Maybe not. Clothing that is labeled 'wrinkle free' or 'easy care' may not be so easy on you. Treatments which make fabrics wrinkle-resistant are typically formaldehyde-based, and can release fumes inside your closet and during the laundry process. As a rule, opt for the most natural fibers you can find, like organic cotton, linen, natural wool (not acrylic blends), bamboo, or hemp. See Resources for a list of retailers, or go to ecomall.com, where you'll find dozens of online resources for natural clothing.

You don't actually like those stinky mothballs, do you? Traditional mothballs contain naphthalene, a registered carcinogen and probably not a substance you want to wear with your favorite sweaters[6]. Instead, repel moths and other creepy-crawlies with natural herb sachets containing rosemary, thyme, American ginseng, cloves, mint leaves, lavender, or cedar. Try **Moth-Away** sachets, available at planetnatural.com, or make your own.

Herbal sachets in your drawers keep your clothes smelling fresh, naturally, so you won't miss those heavily scented laundry products. Herbs like lavender and calendula have natural antimicrobial and disinfectant properties, and they come in all kinds of cute designs. **Cedar Hill Naturals** (cedarhillnaturals.com) sells great refillable sachets for only $4.

NAPHTHALENE is a relative of carcinogenic benzene, and it can alter kidney function. It's extremely toxic to children, and can bioaccumulate in marine organisms, poisoning an entire food chain. You'll find it in mothballs, and also in carpet cleaners and deodorizers.

Speaking of cute ...
We know you love them dearly, but your pets are probably contributing to poor air quality in your bedroom.

bedroom bliss

Pets carry outdoor allergens, pesticides and dander in their fur, and these residues get deposited throughout your home. Attempt to keep pets off your bed by providing them with a nice comfy bed of their own. Minimize the effects of sharing your room with your furry friend by brushing her daily to remove loose fur, and bathing her using a non-toxic, natural pet shampoo as often as possible.

Say no to traditional flea and tick collars. They're full of poisonous chemicals (after all, they're designed to kill things), and they rub off on everything they touch, including you. Check out onlynaturalpets. com and planetnatural.com for less toxic options.

Add a plant! Those plug-in air fresheners pollute your air more than they freshen it: they're full of petroleum derivatives, and their chemical fragrances may irritate sensitive people. Not only do plants help to create a little atmosphere, they're great air cleaners - no plug required!

Plants are nature's air filters, sucking up nasty pollutants like ammonia, formaldehyde, xylene, toluene, acetone, methyl alcohol, carbon monoxide and benzene. And unlike those ionic air filter, plants don't emit ozone as part of the process, only pure oxygen.

All plants are not created equal. These leafy wonders are the best to have in your home:

FICUS
BAMBOO PALM
PEACE LILY

RUBBER PLANT
ENGLISH IVY
BOSTON FERN

SPIDER PLANT
ARECA PALM
LADY PALM

VERVEINE
VERITABLE SAVON
DE MARSEILLE
100% VEGETAL

VIOLE
ITABLE SAVON
E MARSEILLE

VERVEINE
AVON
LE 100% VEGETAL

VIOLE
VERITABLE SAVON
DE MARSEILLE

Did
you know …
**Many bathroom
cleaning product
contain ingredients that
can cause severe upper
respiratory distress,
headaches and even
fainting after
exposure.**

VERVEINE
VERITABLE SAVON
DE MARSEILLE
100% VEGETAL

VIOLE
VERITABLE SAVON
DE MARSEILLE

good bathroom habits

As far as cleanliness goes, you're probably more concerned about your bathroom than any other room in your house. There are probably a half-dozen products under your sink designed to disinfect bathroom surfaces, kill molds and mildew, and generally terrorize every germ in sight. The downside of using products like those is that if they kill germs (read: organic single-celled organisms), they're probably not good for you or your family (read: organic, multi-celled organisms).

If you've ever had to leave the bathroom in the middle of scrubbing the toilet (or shower, or sink) because you felt light-headed from the fumes, you're not a wimp: you've just experienced an acute reaction to your cleaning products! Many bathroom cleaners contain ingredients that can cause reactions like severe upper respiratory distress (i.e. shortness of breath, hyperventilation), headaches, or even fainting after relatively minimal exposure. Some common ingredients in bathroom cleaners are also classified as neurotoxins, reproductive toxins, and carcinogens, and cumulative exposure may cause liver and kidney damage[7].

You don't have to sacrifice your health to keep your bathroom spic and span. Here are some suggestions.

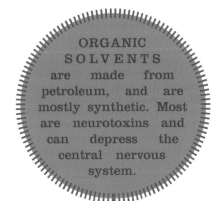

ORGANIC SOLVENTS are made from petroleum, and are mostly synthetic. Most are neurotoxins and can depress the central nervous system.

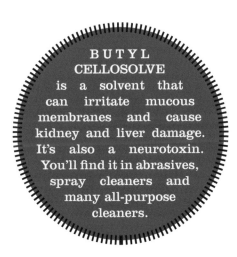

BUTYL CELLOSOLVE is a solvent that can irritate mucous membranes and cause kidney and liver damage. It's also a neurotoxin. You'll find it in abrasives, spray cleaners and many all-purpose cleaners.

For tubs and showers, try a spray cleaner that contains hydrogen peroxide and natural citrus oils to remove stains and soap scum.

Natural Choices OxyBoost Tile Cleaner uses fume-free, non-corrosive oxygen bleach to clean tile and grout (oxyboost.com).

Bon Ami Polishing Cleanser (bonami.com) is another great choice.

Or, just fill a spray bottle with plain white vinegar: this tried-and-true method cuts through soap scum like a charm.

good bathroom habits

Replace commercial toilet bowl cleaners with non-toxic ones. Commercial toilet bowl cleaners are among the most toxic products in your home, and they can cause serious burns if they come in contact with skin and eyes. And don't be fooled into thinking that drop-in bowl cleaners are better: they release toxic fumes continuously into your home, but in small amounts that don't trigger your body's normal protective responses (i.e. headaches, gagging). Natural cleaners use salt-based or enzyme cleaning agents that work just as well as the conventional stuff, without all the potential side effects. Try Ecover's Natural Toilet Bowl Cleaner, recommended by the American Environmental Health Foundation (ecover.com).

Unless your bathroom sees as much traffic as Yankee Stadium, **there's no need to use commercial strength disinfectants on surfaces or floors.** A good weekly scrubbing with a natural cleanser will get your WC as clean as it needs to be.

Conventional tile cleaners are often made with chlorine bleach. Instead, try a tile cleaner with oxygen bleach to get rid of mold and mildew with no harsh fumes or toxic residue.

It's not only your cleaning products that are polluting your bathroom. Vinyl shower curtain liners are some of the worst offenders when it comes to home air pollution. A new liner can emit toxic gases for up to a month. Recent studies have linked the toxins emitted by shower curtain liners and other PVC plastics to cancer and birth defects[8]. If you're remodeling, consider enclosing your shower with glass doors. Otherwise, buy fabric shower curtain liners. They contain fewer chemicals, and since they're machine washable they don't need to be replaced as often.

Concerned about pesticides on your veggies?

Buy organic - and change your cleaning products!

kitchen savvy

It's important to keep kitchen surfaces clean – after all, they're where you prepare your food. But many commercial cleaning products are made with hazardous chemicals which, although they do cut grease and kill germs, can leave chemical residues on your counters, your stove, and your floors. Cleanliness and healthiness don't have to be mutually exclusive. Here are a few ways you can clean up your kitchen cleaners.

Research suggests that up to 60% of substances which contact human skin are absorbed into the body[9]. With that in mind, read the warning labels on most of your kitchen cleaners: you'll never want to walk barefoot across that freshly-washed kitchen floor again. You'll probably reconsider the '5-second rule', too.

Those disinfectant sprays that kill 99.9% of germs on surfaces are actually pesticides[10] masquerading as household helpers! They're marketed as tools to help keep you and your family healhy. But when you spray them in your home, you're actually exposing yourself to a much higher concentration of pesticides than you'll ever find on your veggies. Also worth noting: research has shown that excessive use of antibacterial and disinfectant products can actually harm your immune system, and may contribute to the growth of drug-resistant bacteria and viruses. The bottom line? Unless your immune system is compromised due to a medical condition, you're better off without all those disinfectants.

For floors and surfaces, try a natural cleaner/degreaser with powerful citrus extracts; it'll do the job of your old 'pine' cleaner, and the fumes won't give you a headache. Just be sure to check the ingredients: some commercial products labeled as 'citrus cleaners' are petroleum-based, with very little real citrus oil. Citra-Solv (citra-solv.com) is a nice product, and it's widely available. If you like to use a separate floor cleaner, try Ecover Floor Soap (ecover.com): it's fume-free and pet-safe.

We all love those pop-up cleaning wipes for little messes: no sponge, no rising, no hassle. But commercial cleaning wipes use toxic chemicals like butyl cellusolve, and we don't typically think to wear gloves when we use them (remember the 60% absorption rule?). If wipes are used on surfaces which contact food, it's even worse. Instead, try Method's

EDTA (ethylene-diamino-tetra-acetate) Is used to soften water and to prevent bleaches from activating before the dishwasher starts. In the environment, it can 'reactivate' heavy metals in water and soil, reintroducing poisons into the food chain. It has never been tested for long-term safety in humans.

kitchen savvy

non-toxic, biodegradable cleaning wipes (methodhome.com): they come in great scents like French Lavender.

Another great solution for little messes? Try washable microfiber cleaning cloths. They're easy to find, they last for months, and you can use them with any natural cleaning spray. Used in place of paper towels or cleaning wipes, they can significantly reduce waste – and save you money, too.

Did you know … if everyone in the US bought just one roll of 100% recycled paper towels instead of their usual brand, 544,000 trees and 1.4 million cubic feet of landfill space would be saved! Recycled paper products are available everywhere, and cost the same as (or less than) regular 'virgin' paper products. Check out greenforest-products.com and seventhgeneration.com for where to buy.

Also good to know: If everyone in the US bought just one roll of paper towels whitened without chlorine bleach, it would prevent the release of 38,000 tons of pollutants. Since many 100% recycled paper products are whitened with non-toxic oxygen-based bleaches, you'll be doing double do-gooder duty when you buy recycled[11].

Look for food storage containers that are not made from PVC (polyvinyl chloride), which has been linked to birth defects and cancer. Whole Foods' 365 brand Food Storage Containers are PVC-free, and they're inexpensive. An even better option is to wash and save glass food jars in all shapes and sizes: they're dishwasher safe, non-toxic, and – best of all – free!

Instead of using corrosive drain cleaners, which are among the most hazardous of household chemicals and wreak havoc on the environment, try dissolving greasy clogs by pouring a kettle full of boiling water down the drain. For hair clogs and other messes, try an living culture enzyme cleaner like Bi-O-Kleen's BacOut (biokleenhome.com). The cultures in this cleaner eat away blockages, cause no environmental harm, and are even

17

what's in YOUR dishwasher?

PHOSPHATES, used to soften water and increase detergent effectiveness, are common in commercial dishwashing detergents. While not overtly toxic to humans, they are banned or restricted in many states because they wreak havoc on marine environments by causing explosive algae and microorganism growth.

POLYCARBOXYLATES are the synthetic answer to phosphates. Relatively new, there is no available information about their long term health and environmental effects. What is known is that their chemical structure is similar to plastics and acrylics, they're petroleum based, and they're not biodegradable.

good for your septic system, since they help to 'digest' waste. Another plus: you can use BacOut on your carpets, as a kitchen deodorizer, and even in your fridge.

Commercial oven cleaners – even the 'fume-free' varieties – are highly corrosive and dangerous to skin, eyes, and mucous membranes. Some contain benzene, a known carcinogen and a key item on the EPA's Right to Know list. Acute reactions to inhalation of oven cleaners include pounding headaches and shortness of breath. Plus, any residues left behind get superheated and baked into your food. Sound like fun? I didn't think so. Instead, try scrubbing your oven with baking soda, hot water, and steel wool. Add a little elbow grease, and your oven will be good as new. For really tough stuff, try your citrus degreaser – just be sure to rinse well.

Ever pop open the dishwasher to an eye-stinging blast of steam? **That steam is full of chemicals from your dishwashing detergent** – chemicals like chlorine bleach, EDTA (which has never been tested for long-term health effects), anionic surfactants (which

you'll also find in laundry detergents and floor cleaners), and chemical fragrances (which are added to cover the smells of the other chemicals, and which are subject to little or no formal regulation)(12). Besides being nasty to breathe, these bad guys can hang around on your dishes – so why not try an enzyme based formula? I like Method Dish Cubes (methodhome.com) and Ecover's Automatic Dishwashing Powder (ecover.com), which come in packets so you don't have to measure.

Made from petroleum and coal, BENZENE is classified by the International Agency for Research on Cancer as a carcinogen, is listed in the 1990 Clean Air Act as a hazardous air pollutant, and is on the EPA's Community Right-to-Know list. May be found in conventional oven cleaners, detergents, furniture polish, & spot removers.

THIS AREA
CHEMICALLY TREATED
KEEP CHILDREN
& PETS OFF
UNTIL DRY

family room fundamentals

Remember when Mom had her carpets shampooed, and you couldn't walk through that room for a whole day? There was a good reason for that. Commercial carpet cleaning solutions are highly irritating to skin and mucous membranes, their fumes can be toxic, and they leave chemical residues all over your rugs[13]. But carpet shampoos are not the worst chemical offenders in your family room. That dubious honor goes to the cleaners you use every day. Your floor polishes, commercial dusting sprays, and fabric freshening sprays may be nearly as toxic as the heavy duty stuff – and you use them far more frequently.

To clean carpets: use 1/4 cup oxy bleach in 1 gallon of water in steamers, and 1/4 cup per quart of hot water for spot treatments. OxyClean (oxyclean. com) is available everywhere, and it's fume free: all you'll have to worry about now are your tot's muddy shoes.

Spot clean carpets and upholstery with a natural enzyme-based cleaner. It'll remove pet urine, blood, grass and food stains – and yes, muddy footprints. I like Citra-Solv's Citra Spot Natural Enzymatics (citra-solv.com).

Commercial dusting sprays may contain petroleum byproducts and chemical shine enhancers that you don't want to breathe. **Instead, try diluted castile soap or linseed (flax) oil to clean and shine your wood furniture.** Or, buy a natural preparation: Citrus Magic Wood Soap (citrusmagic.com) with natural lemon oil is safe for all your wood furniture, and it's even good for your skin!

Fabric 'freshener' sprays contain chemical fragrances that can irritate sensitive people. **Freshen tougher fabrics like cotton and wool with a natural linen spray,** which uses essential oils to power away lingering scents. For silk and other delicates, a tumble in a cool to warm dryer with an herbal laundry sachet will usually get rid of musty smells.

Traditional glass cleaners use ammonia and petroleum wax (yes, wax) to give you that 'streak free' shine. **Consider switching to a natural glass cleaner.** Most can be used safely on just

about any surface, so they double as all-purpose cleaners.

Be careful what you burn. Soy candles and natural incense are great alternatives to traditional paraffin candles and plug-in air fresheners – just remember to keep them out of reach of little hands. Or, try fragrance sticks and natural essential oils for a heat-free alternative.

Instead of commercial air fresheners, which use 'liquified, sweetened petroleum gas'[14] to deliver chemical fragrances (yuck!) try a natural non-aerosol air freshener spray with citrus oils.

If the air in your home could really use some help, try zeolite crystals. These natural mineral crystals absorb all kinds of noxious chemicals from the air, including fumes from new carpets, paint, vinyl flooring, and furniture. You can pour crystals in with potted plants, place them in bowls around the house, even hang zeolite 'sachets' in closets, cabinets, and corners. Find more information about zeolite in the EPA report, *Zeolite: A Versatile Air Pollutant Adsorber* at www.epa.gov/ttn/catc/dir1/fzeolite.pdf

Machine-washable microfiber cloths can be used for dry or wet-dusting, and require no chemicals at all.

Magnetic dusters grab up loose particles without needing sprays or sticky products.

OPERATING INSTRUCTIONS

Push red button on handle and pull
Handle to open door.

Load machine. Close door securely.

Put equal amounts of powder in
containers 2 and 3 (Powder bleach
can also be put in container 3)

Put liquid softener (if required)
in container 1

Insert coins into slide, push in
slowly and pull out.

Liquid bleach can be poured in
container 2 when indicator reaches
red position.

3

2

...and don't forget your laundry

You want it all: crisp, clean clothes and a healthy home. You can have both – with a few adjustments to your arsenal of laundry products.

Since your clothes are in direct and constant contact with your skin, it's important to wash them in detergents that don't leave residues. Those 'spring fresh' and 'natural breeze' scented commercial laundry detergents, fabric softeners and dryer sheets are full of petroleum-based surfactants, chemical additives and irritating allergens: there's nothing 'natural' about them. Also, most commercial laundry detergents are non-biodegradable, which means that their chemical ingredients can end up in ground water, lakes, ponds, and eventually our food.

Commercial laundry products can be prime contributors to household air pollution, especially if you wash your clothes in hot water. That fragrant steam wafting out of your washing machine is full of highly concentrated chemicals – and it just hit you full in the face. If you use chlorine bleach on your whites, double the yuck factor. Also, if someone in your household is asthmatic or suffers from a cardiopulmonary condition, bleach fumes can be highly aggravating[15].

Recent studies have shown that fabric softeners and dryer sheets are among the most dangerous products we use in our homes. They contain, among other things: toluene and trimethylbenzene, which are neurotoxins; styrene, a possible carcinogen; phenol and xylene, which are respiratory irritants; and those all-pervasive chemical fragrances. Plus, they're actually meant to leave a thick chemical residue on your clothing as a carrier for that lingering scent, and that residue rubs off on your skin. If you can't forego the fabric softener altogether, try Mrs. Meyers Clean Day Geranium dryer sheets (mrsmeyers.com) or Method's Softener-Infused Dryer Sheets (methodhome.com); they're non-toxic and biodegradable.

Whenever possible, avoid dry-cleaning your clothes. It's estimated that 75% of American dry cleaners use the solvent perchlorethylene (PERC), a potential carcinogen, neurotoxin, and liver toxin which has recently been banned in California[16]. Studies have shown that the fumes from dry-cleaned clothes can pollute a whole room, even an entire house. When confined

ALKYL PHENOXY POLYETHOXY ETHANOLS These synthetic surfactants are common in conventional laundry detergents. English researchers found that even traces of these chemicals activate estrogen receptors in cells, which can alter gene activity and contribute to all manner of health problems.

If you must dry clean your clothing, and can't find an ecologically responsible dry cleaner who doesn't use PERC, remove the dry-cleaned items from their plastic bags and leave them on a porch or in the garage to air out before bringing them into your house.

...and don't forget your laundry

to a small space like a closet, they can cause acute toxic reactions. There is some good news, though: as more information about PERC becomes available, many drycleaners are switching to less-toxic cleaning solutions. To find a green dry cleaner in your area, go to greenearthcleaning.com/rostersearch.asp.

Save your skin! Natural, non-toxic laundry detergents won't aggravate skin conditions or respiratory ailments. They smell great, rinse clean, and are highly concentrated. If you have allergies or very sensitive skin, try an unscented, dye-free formula like Seventh Generation's Free and Clear Laundry Powder (seventhgeneration.com).

Instead of chlorine bleach, try non-toxic hydrogen peroxide bleach. It's color-safe, odorless, and has dozens of other household uses. Best of all, it's safe for groundwater, septic systems, the environment, and your family. Ecover (ecover.com) makes a great liquid non-chlorine bleach. Powdered oxygen bleaches are handy too: make a concentrated solution to pretreat stains, or soak stained clothes prior to washing.

Try an enzyme-based stain remover instead of a commercial preparation. They're safe for most fabrics and lift out just about anything.

Herbal laundry sachets, like those from Sweetgrass Farm (sweetgrassonline.com) **can be tossed in the dryer** with your damp clothes to add fragrance without softening agents.

KEEP YOUR COOL

Wash clothes in cold water whenever possible. Not only is it actually better for most fabrics, it saves energy too!

non-toxic nurseries

We all want the world for our children. We want to protect them in every possible way, and give them the best of everything. But in doing so, we should be cautious about the products we choose for them: many of the products geared toward babies and young children are unsafe, and potentially toxic. This issue was brought to the forefront of the public consciousness by the recent scare over imported toys – but lead paint is not the only culprit that conscientious parents should be wary of.

In the following pages, I hope to help you prepare a safe sanctuary for your baby or toddler. Not only will I explain how to clean the nursery and its contents healthfully – previous chapters have already discussed most of the products you'll be using – I'll show you how to prepare, decorate, and furnish the nursery or playroom using eco-friendly, non-toxic materials.

If you're an expectant parent – or if you hope to be expecting soon – this chapter will help you as well: when your bundle of joy arrives, you'll be confident that home is as safe as it can be. If you're already a parent, please don't think it's too late - or that you have to tear apart your existing nursery. Simply make a list of items that you want to change or eliminate, and begin to take baby steps. Remember that creating a safe, non-toxic home is not a one-time event: it's a process which will eventually become a lifestyle. You're already on the right path.

The greatest gift you can give your child is the gift of health. Even if you don't have children, you probably know folks who do: please share this information with them, so we can all help to make the world a safer, more healthful place for the next generation.

EASY ON THE EARTH, EASY ON YOUR BUDGET

Check thrift stores for a wealth of used furnishings perfect for your nursery. Furnishings can be reupholstered with beautiful untreated fabrics, and refinished with non-toxic paints and stains. With a minimum of time and effort, you'll have a nursery full of beautiful, one-of-a-kind custom pieces that you – and baby – will enjoy for years to come.

non-toxic nurseries

Avoid traditional paints in the nursery, especially oil-based paints. The new low-VOC paints available from many manufacturers come in loads of cute colors, and release far fewer toxins into the air[17]. See Resources for companies.

When choosing baby furniture, stick to pieces made from solid hardwood, as items made from particleboard and plywood may be treated with formaldehyde and other chemicals. Also, look for non-toxic paint or stain finishes (especially if you're buying imported furnishings). Hardwood furnishings may be pricier, but they're safest for baby and the earth, and unlike their plastic or plywood counterparts, they'll probably last long enough to become family heirlooms. Check out oeufnyc.com and ducducnyc.com for eco-cool furniture, accessories, and other objects of desire.

When designing your nursery, you'll probably be looking for parent-sized furniture too. Fear not: lots of cool companies are springing up to meet the growing demand for eco-conscious furniture made from natural, minimally processed materials. Check out el-furniture.com, ciscobrothers.com and vivavi.com, all great sources for stylish green furnishings. If you're skeptical, turn to the old standards: Amish and Mennonite artisans have been making eco-conscious, chemical-free furniture for generations. If Lancaster, PA isn't your next vacation destination, check out these web pages: anaturalhome.com and amishloft.com.

Wood, linoleum, and tile are much healthier flooring choices than carpeting – especially in a nursery, where baby will likely spend a good deal of time on or close to the floor. That 'new carpet' smell is caused by chemical out-gassing of the synthetic carpet fibers, and fumes can be toxic as well as irritating to sensitive respiratory tracts[18]. Vinyl floors are also a big no-no; they're made with a variant of PVC, and emit their own brand of toxic fumes[19]. Soften hard flooring surfaces with throw rugs in natural fibers like wool or silk, and clean often. If you can't do away with the wall-to-wall, a natural carpet sealant like SafeChoice can help lock away toxins. Learn more at afmsafecoat.com

When buying toys, make sure they're made from safe materials. Recent lead paint scares have really raised awareness, but unfortunately lead paint isn't the only toxic component found in baby and toddler products. Many baby and toddler toys are made from toxic PVC – as are teething rings, crib liners, and other items. PVC (a.k.a. vinyl), in all its many incarnations, has been linked to cancers, birth defects, and other ailments[20]. Its manufacture wreaks havoc on the environment, and it cannot be recycled as other plastics can. Instead of plastic toys, look for stuffed toys made from organic cotton, and natural wood toys finished with non-toxic paints. Check out islandtreasuretoys.com and egiggle.com for great toys and gifts, and see Resources for where to find more info on PVC.

non-toxic nurseries

Do you really know what your little one is sleeping in? Your baby will be spending the next few years snuggled up in their crib, so choose bedding wisely. Traditional mattresses are treated with chemicals like formaldehyde to make them stain-resistant and flame-retardant[21]. There are even tentative links between the chemicals used in baby bedding and Sudden Infant Death Syndrome (SIDS)[22]. You can find reasonably priced organic cotton and wool crib mattresses at furnature.com and at abundantearth.com.

Would you eat that? Instead of using disinfectant wipes or sprays on baby toys, wash them in hot water with a mild castile soap – like Dr. Bronner's Magic Soap (drbronner.com) – which won't leave residues for baby to chew on. If toys can go in the dishwasher, make sure your dishwashing powder is free of bleach, petroleum by-products and other inedible stuff. Earthwise Liquid Laundry Detergent freshens using natural grapefruit and eucalyptus (earthwiseshop.co.nz).

When you change baby's toys, change what you put them in, too. Organize and store baby toys in natural fiber baskets or cloth bags where possible. If plastic bins are a must, let them 'breathe' outside for a day or so before bringing them into the house, and wash them well with mild soap and water before filling them with toys.

When possible, choose organic cotton crib sheets, mattress covers, blankets, and comforters. Many conventional baby linens are treated with chemicals to make them stain-resistant, colorfast, and fire-retardant[23]. Also, avoid polyester and other synthetics. If you have your heart set on a particular fabric that's not certified organic, check out SafeWash at furnature.com; it's a handy service which removes chemical finishes and dye odors from fabrics. Also, remember to wash baby bedding in laundry detergents that don't contain petroleum byproducts or chemical fragrances, and never use conventional dryer sheets or fabric softeners.

back to basics

Times have changed since the days of laundry tubs and washboards. Advances in science and technology have provided us with modern conveniences like microwave ovens and dishwashers, washing machines and clothes dryers. It's hard to imagine life without these time-saving devices – and as our lives have become filled with work, travel, family obligations, and commuting hours, it's become impossible to do without them. But some of our modern advances are not so wonderful – like our dependence on unnatural chemicals, plastics, and 'throwaway' products.

While I'm not suggesting that we return to the days of washboards and wood-burning cookstoves, I do think that we can learn a lot from our grandmothers and great-grandmothers when it comes to cleaning. I'm a big fan of green cleaning products, but I know that the cost of these products can be a disincentive to many consumers. Also, nontoxic products may be hard to find in some areas. Therefore, I'm devoting this chapter to the rediscovery of what our grandmothers and great-grandmothers knew: you don't need chemicals to keep your home spotless and shining. All you need are the Fab Five!

The ingredients I've dubbed the Fab Five – hydrogen peroxide, lemon juice, white vinegar, baking soda, and castile soap – are ingredients which women (and men) have used to clean their homes since the days of our forefathers. These ingredients are cheap, readily available, and totally effective. And, best of all, they really do work: I've tried every one of the techniques in this chapter in my own home, with incredible results. So read on for tried-and-true, thoroughly non-toxic, totally fab tips and tricks – and Clean Your Home Healthy, the old-fashioned way!

back to basics

Mildew and mold can creep up on you, infesting stored linens and clothing. Add a cup of white vinegar to your non-toxic laundry detergent to power out musty smells and mildew stains.

Castile soap is great for spot-cleaning soiled clothes, and can even be used in place of your existing laundry detergent. Use ¼ to ⅓ cup per load. It's great for underwear and sheets, since it leaves no irritating residues. Also, adding ⅓ to ½ cup of baking soda per load makes castile soap even more effective.

To get rid of sweat stains on your clothing, rub a paste of baking soda and water into the stain an hour or two before washing. This trick also works on fruit and wine stains, especially if you apply the paste when the stain is fresh.

Deodorize stinky shoes with baking soda. Just sprinkle it right into shoes at night, then tap it out in the morning. For leather or suede shoes, which can become brittle if a buildup of baking soda accumulates, make shoe sachets: cut the toes from an old pair of pantyhose or cotton socks and stuff them with baking soda, then tie off the open ends to make some mean odor-eaters! For even more deodorizing power, mix the baking soda with antimicrobial herbs like lavender, sage, and rosemary.

IN THE BATHROOM

A solution of white vinegar in hot water is a great cleaner for all bathroom surfaces. Use ½ cup to 1 cup of vinegar per gallon of water for tubs, tile, floors, sinks, and even mirrors.

Mildew can't stand up to good old white vinegar. Spray your shower, tub, and tile with full-strength vinegar, let stand, then wipe clean. Also, remember that prevention is the best defense: mildew and soap scum thrive on moist surfaces, so keep a squeegee handy to swipe shower doors after each use, and stash a bucket of rags under the sink to wipe basins and faucets.

Lemon juice, used full-strength, powers through soap scum on faucets, shower doors, and tile. It also dissolves hard water deposits, and leaves your loo smelling fresh.

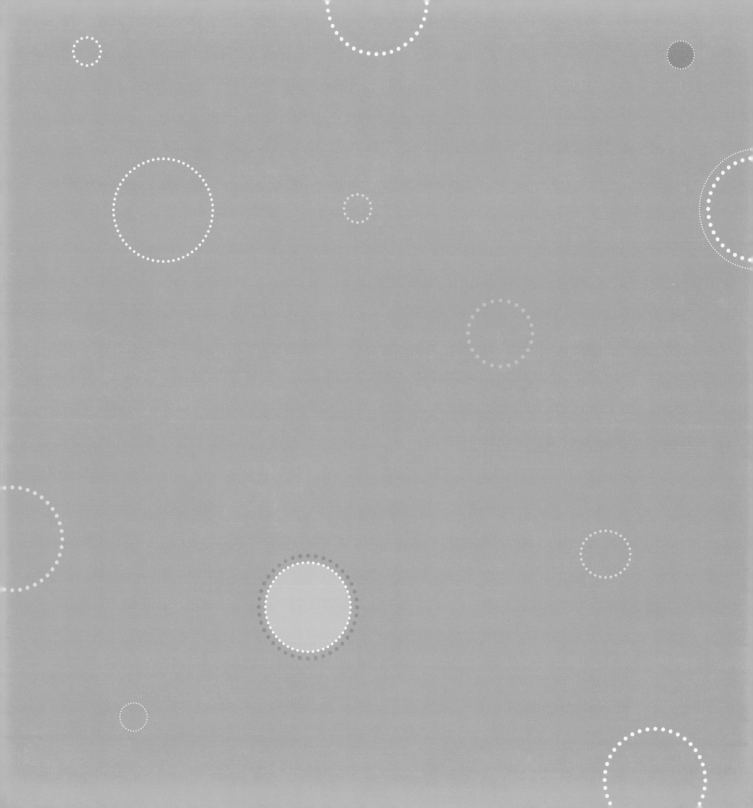

back to basics

Solve your soap-scum problems by switching to castile soap at the sink and in the shower: it's great for your skin and the earth, and doesn't leave a hardened residue on any surface.

KITCHEN

A mild solution of castile soap (1 part soap to 40 parts water) makes a terrific all-purpose cleaner. Use it on floors, walls, appliances, everywhere you'd use your commercial spray cleaner.

Use castile soap in place of your current dish liquid. It leaves no residue, and gets glass and silverware bright.

Undiluted lemon juice cleans and shines brass and copper. Just slice a fresh lemon in half and scrub away. Or, try this formula: Sprinkle baking soda onto your copper-bottom pans, spritz with white vinegar, and then scrub the whole foamy mix into the pans with a fresh lemon half. Just be sure to rinse pans thoroughly.

To clean roasting pans and cookie sheets, sprinkle baking soda onto the pan, then pour on a solution of 1 cup hot water and $1/3$ cup vinegar. The fizzing action will clear away baked-on food particles.

An open carton of baking soda in the fridge absorbs odors like a sponge.

Got a clogged drain? Make a volcano! If you (or your children) have ever concocted an erupting volcano for a science class, you'll appreciate this: sprinkle baking soda down your temperamental drain, then follow with a shot of white vinegar to foam away buildup.

Vinegar is not only powerful, it's deadly - to germs, that is! Studies have shown that good old white vinegar can wipe out bacteria, molds, and viruses when applied to surfaces[24]. How? Vinegar is acidic, and microorganisms simply can't thrive in an overly acidic environment. But, unlike with commercial antibacterial products, there are no chemical pesticides involved, so there's no chance of bacterial mutation, and no effect on human or animal immune systems. If you're fresh out of white vinegar, you can use apple cider vinegar or wine vinegar in its place – just be careful on white or pale surfaces.

back to basics

To disinfect countertops and cutting boards, spray full-strength vinegar onto the surface and let stand for at least 10 minutes before rinsing. Or, spritz just before bedtime, and leave overnight. The vinegar scent dissipates within an hour or so, and you'll wake up to a sanitized, healthy kitchen.

White vinegar, diluted with hot water, can be used on floors, stoves, windows, and most other kitchen surfaces. A solution of ¼ cup baking soda, ½ cup vinegar, and 1 gallon of water will degrease and deodorize appliances and floors. One caveat: since it dissolves calcium-based stone and deposits (like hard water stains), vinegar should never be used on marble, dolomite, or limestone. When cleaning your stone surfaces, stick to a natural all-purpose cleaner, or use castile soap and hot water.

FAMILY ROOM

Baking soda is the ultimate deodorizer. To get pet odors out of carpets, sprinkle baking soda on your rugs, let it sit for a few minutes, then vacuum up.

Hydrogen peroxide is great for getting stains out of everything; it's the basis of natural non-chlorine bleaches. You can use a diluted solution of peroxide to remove stains from rugs and upholstery – just test a small, invisible area of fabric first, to ensure colorfastness.

Vinegar and warm water: it's the age-old formula for glass cleaning, and it's still effective. However, your commercial glass cleaners might be leaving waxy residues behind, so before you begin your vinegar cleaning routine, spritz mirrors and other glass surfaces with a mixture of ½ cup white vinegar and 1tsp. castile soap (or your current dish soap) in 2 cups of hot water. Take five deep breaths (no fumes!), then wipe off.

IN THE NURSERY

Castile soap is great for laundering diaper covers, baby linens, and baby clothes, since it leaves no irritating residues. Use ¼ to $^1/_3$ cup per load in place of your normal detergent. Don't use it on cloth diapers, though, since it may interfere with the way

back to basics

the cloth absorbs liquid – instead, use a natural detergent and/or baking soda to get diapers spotless.

Crib mattress covers, changing pads, and other baby linens may benefit from periodic washing in hot water and white vinegar, to power out lingering stains and odors.

Get baby spit-up stains out of clothes and other fabrics by applying a paste of baking soda and water to items an hour before laundering.

Clean baby's toys with castile soap and hot water. A solution of vinegar and water is a great way to disinfect plastic toys, and won't leave behind any residues for baby to chew on.

PRODUCTS TO TRUST

White Vinegar: Heinz sells their white vinegar by the gallon, and it's cheap.

Lemon juice: Fresh, whole lemons are best; natural enzymes are lost through the pasteurization process, making bottled juice far less effective. If you want to be truly eco-conscious, buy local and/or organic lemons where possible.

Hydrogen Peroxide: You can find it in natural oxygen bleaches, like Ecover's Liquid Non-chlorine Bleach (ecover.com), or just buy it straight up by the quart or by the gallon. A 3% solution is standard: anything more concentrated may be harsh on skin.

Baking Soda: Arm and Hammer is the old standard, and the easiest to find. Buy in bulk: it's easier on your wallet, and easier on the earth since it uses less packaging.

Castile Soap: Dr. Bronner's Magic Soaps (drbronner.com) are easy to find, highly concentrated, and relatively inexpensive when you consider how little you actually need to use. They're great for cleaning, and also in the shower and at the sink in place of your regular soap. The scented varieties use organic essential oils.

when you're done...

Many of us fool ourselves into thinking that when we put the garbage out on the curb and the garbage man puts it on the truck, that it disappears forever. In a perfect world, this would be true. But in our world, everyone's trash has to go somewhere – and it's piling up in our landfills, our rivers, and our oceans at an alarming rate.

Plastics create one of the biggest disposal problems we face in today's world. Plastic biodegrades at a snail's pace, over the course of tens of thousands of years. Some researchers say that it never truly goes away at all, that it only breaks down into smaller and smaller pieces which wreak environmental havoc when they enter the food chain. What every researcher seems to agree upon is the fact that every piece of plastic ever manufactured is still in existence – except those which have been incinerated, and are now polluting our air and water in a different way.

Recycling is one of the most important things you can do to help our planet. Not only is it an integral part of Green Cleaning, it's easy and convenient, and chances are you do it already. Not every plastic can be recycled (yet), but a good number of the ones we use every day can be, and should be. So when you've finished up those bottles of conventional cleaners, please be sure to dispose of them correctly.

For reference purposes, here's a list of plastics by recycling code number. Note that PVC, one of the dangerous plastics discussed in earlier chapters, is labeled #3. This makes it easy to check products before you buy.

Each of the three arrows represents a step in a three-step recycling loop.

The process begins with the collection of materials to be recycled. The first arrow represents recyclable materials placed in your curbside bin or taken to a local collection center. Collected materials are cleaned and sorted for sale to a manufacturing facility. The second arrow represents the manufacturing process, when the recyclable materials are re-manufactured into new products for retail or wholesale. The third arrow represents the purchase and use of products made from the recycled materials.

PETE

HDPE

V

LDPE

PP

PS

OTHER

#1 - **PETE** (Polyethylene Terephthalate): a type of polyester used in plastic soda and water bottles, medicine bottles, etc.

#2 - **Polyethylene**: a heavier type of polymer used in the bottles most household products are packaged in. Also used in some grocery bags and toys.

#3 - **PVC** (Polyvinyl Chloride): used in toys, baby bottle nipples, household plumbing, raincoats, vinyl siding, plastic food wrap, and car dashboards, to name a few.

#4 - **Low Density Polyethylene**: used in grocery bags, sandwich bags, and other filmy-type plastic products.

#5 - **Polypropylene**: found in some food containers (like yogurt containers and syrup bottles), outdoor carpeting, and disposable diapers.

#6 - **Polystyrene** (a.k.a. Styrofoam): most commonly used in packing 'peanuts', as well as in coffee cups and meat trays.

#7 - **Other**: includes resins not mentioned above or combinations of plastics.

Currently, only #1 and #2 plastics can be recycled at most facilities, although programs for collecting plastic grocery bags and other #4 plastics are becoming more common. When you're transitioning into your green cleaning routine, take a moment to throw that clean, empty plastic bottle in your recycle bin, and you'll be doing even more to help the planet.

companies to love

Cleaning and Laundry Products

Bi-O-Kleen Industries
Household cleaners, laundry products
P.O. Box 820689
Vancouver, WA 98682
Toll Free: 800-477-018
www.biokleenhome.com

Bon-Ami
Household cleaners
510 Walnut, Suite 300
Kansas City, MO 64106-1209
www.bonami.com

Citra-Solv
Household cleaners, laundry products
Also furniture care products, air fresheners
P.O. Box 2597
Danbury, CT 06813-2597
Phone: 203-778-0881
www.citra-solv.com

Citrus Magic
Household cleaners, laundry products, soaps,
air fresheners, automotive products, pet
products
www.citrusmagic.com

Clean Environment Company
Household cleaners, laundry products, pet
care products
www.cleanenvironmentco.com

Dr. Bronner's Magic Soaps
Natural castile soaps, body care
P.O. Box 28
Escondido, CA 92033
760-743-2211
www.drbronner.com

Earthwise Direct Ltd.
Household cleaners, laundry products, hair
and body care, baby care, plant care
134 Riverlea Road Hillcrest
Hamilton, New Zealand
Phone: +64 (07) 859 3410
www.earthwiseshop.co.nz

Ecover
One of the longest-established manufacturers
of natural and non-toxic household cleaners
and laundry products.
Toll free: 800-449-4925
www.ecover.com

Green Forest Products
Recycled and eco-friendly household paper
products
P.O. Box 48184
3575 Douglas Street
Victoria, BC Canada V8Z 7H6
Phone: 888-478-8131
www.greenforest-products.com

Method
Household cleaners, laundry products

637 Commercial Street
San Francisco, CA 94111
Phone: 415-931-3947 or 866-9-METHOD
www.methodhome.com

Mrs. Meyer's Clean Day
Household cleaners, laundry products
Also pet products, candles
Phone: 877-865-1508
www.mrsmeyers.com

Natural Choices
Oxygen bleaches, household cleaners, laundry
products, furniture cleaners
9525 South 60th Street
Franklin, WI 53132
Phone: 866-OXY-BOOST
www.oxyboost.com

Organica Biotech
Household cleaners
Also gardening and water gardening products
705 General Washington Avenue, Suite 500
Norristown, PA 19403
Phone: 888-24-GREEN
www.organica.net

Oxy-Clean (Church & Dwight Company)
Oxygen bleach for laundry and household
cleaning
469 N. Harrison St.
Princeton, NJ 08540
Phone: 800-781-7529
www.oxyclean.com

Seventh Generation
Household cleaners, laundry products, paper
products

60 Lake Street
Burlington, VT 05401-5218
Phone: 800-456-1191 or 802-658-3773
www.seventhgeneration.com

Simple Green/Sunshine Makers, Inc.
Household cleaners
15922 Pacific Coast Highway
Huntington Harbor, CA 92649
Phone: 800-228-0709
www.simplegreen.com

Sun and Earth
Household cleaners, laundry products, soaps,
microfiber cleaning cloths
125 Noble Street
Norristown, PA 19401
Phone: 800-298-7861
www.sunandearth.com

Sweetgrass Farm
Laundry products, soaps, candles, bath and
body products
16 Alden Ave
Greenland, NH 03840
Phone: 603-766-1651
www.sweetgrassonline.com

Candles and Incense

Eternal Lites, Inc.
Lead-free cotton wicks, non-alcohol fragrances
Also fragrance oils and diffuser lamps
2574 Merrick Road
Bellmore, NY 11710
Phone: 516-781-7818
www.eternallites.com

Maddison Avenue Candle Company
Natural soy candles. Custom-designed candles
19530 ECR 330 N
Charleston, IL 61920
www.maddisonavenue.net

Shadow and Light, Inc.
Soy Candles
Available at retailers and at several internet
stores including:
www.sensia.com
www.aromatherapycandle.com
www.candlefind.com

Online Retail Resources

www.abundantearth.com
Furniture, gifts, air purifiers, personal care

www.ecomall.com
Online mall featuring everything green, from
cleaning products to clothing to services, with
links to dozens of retailers' web pages.

www.myorganichouse.com
retails PureRest organic cotton sheets and
pillowcases, and other organic home goods.

www.naturallygood.net
Organic cotton sheets, blankets, duvets, and
bedding free of formaldehyde finishes and
dioxins from bleaching.

www.naturebaby.com
Online store with everything baby, from cleaners
to clothes to diapers.

www.nontoxiclife.com
Online store with a great selection of cleaners
and home products.

www.planetnatural.com
Natural insect repellents, lawn care, gardening
and home products.

www.sensia.com
Shadow and Light soy candles, incense bath
and body products

www.villagegreenmarket.com
Online store featuring a good selection of
candles, cleaning products, and personal care.

www.vivaterra.com
organic cotton, silk, bamboo, and maize
bedding, and luxury natural home goods.

www.wholisticplanetstore.com
a complete line of organic cotton damask
bedding, plus lots more.

Non-toxic Nurseries

Abundant Earth, Inc.
Crib mattresses, baby care, toys, and more
Phone: 800-51-EARTH
www.abundantearth.com

Dr. Bronner's Magic Soaps
Natural castile soaps, body care
P.O. Box 28
Escondido, CA 92033
Phone: 760-743-2211
www.drbronner.com

DucDuc, LLC
Natural baby furniture, textiles and accessories
524 Broadway # 206
New York, NY 10012
Phone: 877-5-DUCDUC or 212-226-1868
www.ducducnyc.com

Giggle
Clothing, toys, furniture and more
Phone: 800-495-8577
www.egiggle.com

Furnature
Carries organic cotton and wool crib mattresses,
and furniture for the entire home
86 Coolidge Avenue
Watertown, MA 02472
Phone: 800-326-4895
www.furnature.com

Island Treasure Toys
A great selection of natural wood toys
359 Main Street
Yarmouth, MA 04096
Phone: 888-794-5388
www.islandtreasuretoys.com

Oeuf, LLC
Baby furniture, loungers and clothing
323 6th Street Suite #4
Brooklyn, NY 11215
Phone: 800-691-8810
www.oeufnyc.com

Nurseries - green remodeling

Benjamin Moore, Inc.
Eco-Spec paints are solvent-free
www.benjaminmoore.com for retailers
Green Planet Paints
Natural, zero-VOC paints made with mineral
pigments. They can also help you find the best
ingredients to mix your own paints.
P.O. Box 13
Patagonia, AZ 85264
Phone: 520-394-2571
www.greenplanetpaints.com

ECOS Organic Paints (UK)
Natural, solvent and VOC free paints
Unit 34 Heysham Business Park, Middleton
Road, Heysham, Lancashire LA3 3PP
Phone: 00 44 (0) 1524 852371
www.ecospaints.com

The Real Milk Paint Company
Organic paint as a water-soluble powder
suitable for furniture and restoration
11 West Pumping Station Road
Quakertown, PA 18951
Phone: 800-339-9748 or
215-538-3886
www.realmilkpaint.com

Cisco Brothers
Collections and made-to-measure furniture
consciously constructed.
Stores in CA and NY
www.ciscobrothers.com

Environmental Language Furniture
Modern eco-friendly furnishings
425 Park Barrington Drive,
Barrington, IL 60010
Phone: 847-382-9285
www.el-furniture.com

Furnature
Natural furniture for eco-savvy or chemically
sensitive consumers
86 Coolidge Avenue
Watertown, MA 02472
Phone: 800-326-4895
www.furnature.com

The Organic Mattress Store
Mattresses, futons, cribs – even pet beds
Showroom: 410 Main Street
Hellertown, PA 18055
Phone: 484-851-3636
www.theorganicmattressstore.com

Vivavi
Modern eco-friendly furnishings
644 Manhattan Ave 2nd Floor
Brooklyn, NY 11222
Phone: 866-848-2840
www.vivavi.com

Zola Eco-Friendly Furnishings
Natural eco-friendly and sustainable heirloom
quality furnishings
1320 SE Armour Dr. STE B-1 Bend, OR
97702
Phone: 866-450-1457
www.zolafurnishings.com

Green Remodeling Resources

www.eartheasy.com
advice, suggestions, studies and articles, and
links to earth-friendly sites and retailers.

www.lowimpactliving.com
Advice, suggestions, newsletters, and links
to retailers and resources. You can find green
architects and interior designers listed here,
and their February 2007 newsletter is all about
green remodeling. Here's the link:
www.lowimpactliving.com/newsletter/
newsletter_green%20kitchen%2022Feb2007.
htm

www.shopbluehouse.com
A huge online shop for everything an eco-
friendly home needs, including furniture,
linens, personal care, flooring and accessories.

www.thegreenguide.com
An online resource and printed 12 page
newsletter recently acquired by National
Geographic. A great database, objective
research and reviews, and information about
every aspect of 'green' living.

resources

<u>Organic Housekeeping: In Which the Non-Toxic Avenger Shows You How to Improve Your Health and That of Your Family, While You Save Time, Money, and, Perhaps, Your Sanity</u> (Hardcover) By Ellen Sandbeck, 2006. Published by Scribner.

<u>The Complete Organic Pregnancy</u> (Hardcover) by Dierdre Dolan and Alexandra Zissu, 2006. Published by Harper Collins

<u>The Healthy Home Workbook: Easy Steps for Eco-friendly Living</u>, by Kimberly Rider. Photographed by Thayer Allyson Gowdy, 2006. Published by Chronicle Books.

organizations' web pages

www.aehf.com
American Environmental Health Foundation
Articles, products and resources

www.cancer.org
American Cancer Society
Information, articles, contacts

www.healthychild.org
Healthy Child, Healthy World

resources, articles and information

12300 Wilshire Boulevard, Suite 320
Los Angeles, CA 90025
Phone: 310-820-2030

www.earth911.com
Information, local resources, events and contacts

www.ewg.org
Environmental Working Group
Independent testing group, articles, links and resources

www.foe.co.uk
Friends of the Earth
Shopping, information, resources

www.fromnaturewithlove.com
Supplier of natural ingredients to be used in bath and body, aromatherapy, massage, and candlemaking. Also features books, equipment, and information

www.greenguide.com
Info, articles, and resources for home design and remodeling

www.greenpeace.org
The International Greenpeace site -

Information about products, practices and pollution that impact the world's citizens

www.greenseal.org
Green Seal
Independent non-profit organization issuing environmental certification and eco-safety standards to products. Website has a list of companies who meet standards for approval.

www.nrdc.org
National Resources Defense Council
Information and Resources

www.safemilk.org
Make Our Milk Safe (MOMS)
Information, articles and resources for concerned mothers

www.ucsusa.com
Union of Concerned Scientists
Information and resources, newsletter available. National Headquarters:
2 Brattle Square
Cambridge, MA 02238-9105
Phone: 617-547-5552

U.S. EPA's Right To Know List
www.epa.gov/epahome/r2k.htm

www.atsdr.cdc.gov
Agency for Toxic Substances and Disease Registry

www.cdc.gov
Centers for Disease Control

www.chemistry.org
American Chemical Society

www.health.gov
consumer health issues web page

www.neha.org
National Environmental Health Association

www.nih.gov
National Institute of Health

www.nsc.org
National Safety Council

www.hhs.gov
U.S. Department of Health and Human Services

www.epa.gov
U.S. Environmental Protection Agency

references

Room by Room

(1) For stats and info, visit the American Association of Poison Control Centers at www.aapcc.org

Bedroom Bliss

(2) Info on cotton production practices: Sustainable Cotton Project at www.sustainablecotton.org

(3) Formaldehyde in fabrics
a. National Geographic's Green Guide website www.greenguide.com
b. Lotus Organics article: *Wake Up and Smell the Formaldehyde*
www.lotusorganics.com/articles/Formaldehyde.aspx
c. National Cancer Institute Fact Sheet, Formaldehyde and Cancer: Questions and Answers
www.cancer.gov/cancertopics/factsheet/Risk/formaldehyde
d. Childrens Health Environmental Coalition (CHEC) article, *Chemical Profile: Formaldehyde*
www.checnet.org/healthehouse/chemicals/chemicals-detail2.asp?Main_ID=346

(4) Natural vs. synthetic bedding
a. Article: *Creating the Healthy, Sustainable Bedroom* by Mary Cordaro at www.h3environmental.com/learn
b. Blackwell Synergy posted article: *Permeability of Synthetic and Feather Pillows to Live House Dust Mites and House Dust* by R. Siebers, H.S. Nam and J. Crane
www.blackwell-synergy.com/doi/abs/10.1111/j.1365-2222.2004.01972.x?cookieSet=1&journalCode=cea
c. Info on organic bedding at www.goodnightnaturals.com/learn.htm
d. Time Magazine article: *Sleep Goes Green,* by Coeli Carr, Jan-12-07
www.time.com/time/magazine/article/0,9171,1576849,00.html

(5) Paraffin wax emits 11 toxins
a. Find a number of articles posted on the Maddison Avenue Candles site at www.maddisonavenue.net/why_soy_wax_candles.htm: scroll down to heading, 'other articles'
b. Timothy Han article: *Toxins Associated with Paraffin Wax*. Also useful links to EPA articles
www.timothyhan.com/soycandles/paraffin.cfm;
c. Timothy Han, *Toxins Associated with Artificial Scents*
www.timothyhan.com/soycandles/scents.cfm. For more on fragrances, visit the Immune Web site at www.immuneweb.org/articles/fragrancelist.html

(6) Naphthalene in mothballs
a. *Illness Associated with Naphthalene in Mothballs*, MMWR Weekly, 1-23-1983 (through CDC web page)
www.cdc.gov/mmwr/preview/mmwrhtml/00001236.htm
b. Also of interest: Children's Health Environmental Coalition (CHEC) article: *Chemical Summary, Naphthalene*
www.checnet.org/healthehouse/chemicals/chemicals-detail2.asp?Main_ID=292
c. Information excerpted from *Toxocological Profile for Naphthalene December 1990 Agency for Toxic Substances and Disease Registry United States Public Health Service*, posted on eco-usa:
www.eco-usa.net/toxics/naph.shtml
d. You can also find information in on mothballs and safe alternatives in The Complete Organic Pregnancy by Dierdre Dolan and Alexandra Zissu. See Resources for full book info.

Good Bathroom Habits

(7) Bathroom cleaners contain neurotoxins, chlorine, etc.
a. *How Toxic are Your Household Cleaning Supplies?* On the Organic Consumers Association website:
www.organicconsumers.org/articles/article_279.cfm
b. Look up your particular brand of cleaner in the Household Products Database at www.householdproducts.nlm.nih.gov/products.htm. There, you'll find links to TOXNET and PubMed studies and articles.

(8) Vinyl shower curtains outgas one month or more
a. www.greenpeace.org for more than a dozen articles on polyvinyl chloride. See the list at www.greenpeace.org/international/news?related_item_id=89384.
Also, *PVC: The Poison Plastic*, in the Greenpeace archives at www.archive.greenpeace.org/toxics/html/content/pvc1.html
b. Washington Toxics Coalition article, *Vinyl Exam: Eliminating PVC in Your Home* by Phillip Dickey
www.watoxics.org/files/vinyl.pdf
c. The Complete Organic Pregnancy, by Dierdre Dolan and Alexandra Zissu - See Resources for
book info.

Kitchen Savvy

(9) Up to 60% of substances on skin are absorbed into the body
a. Environmental Working Group's Skin Deep study www.ewg.org/skindeep
b. Campaign for Safe Cosmetics: www.safecosmetics.org/newsroom for articles

(10) Disinfectant sprays as pesticides
a. EPA web site articles *What are Antimicrobial Pesticides?*
www.epa.gov/oppad001/ad_info.htm, and *Antimicrobial Pesticide Products*
www.epa.gov/pesticides/factsheets/antimic.htm
b. Childrens Health Environmental Coalition (CHEC) article: *Antibacterials and Disinfectants: Are They Necessary?* S. Hartman
www.checnet.org/healthehouse/education/

articles-detail.asp?Main_ID=121
(11) Stats on paper products
a. Seventh Generation gathers stats for each of its products: see www.seventhgeneration.com/making_difference/consumer_education.php
b. www.buyrecycled.com/questions.htm
c. Read an excerpt from Paul Hawken's The Ecology of Commerce, A Declaration of Sustainability at www.dolphinblue.com/whybuy.html

(12) Harmful ingredients in dishwashing detergents (chlorine, EDTA, fragrances)
a. Look up the ingredients in your product in the Household Products Database: www.householdproducts.nlm.nih.gov/products.htm
b. Article: *Identify Unhealthy Household Cleaners*, Reader's Digest RD Living web page www.rd.com/content/identify-unhealthy-household-cleaners/

Family Room Fundamentals

(13) Carpet shampoo and cleaners
a. Info on carpet care and air quality www.lung.ca. Click on Air Quality: Protect Your Lungs
b. Children's Health Environmental Coalition (CHEC) articles: *Are Carpet Cleaners Safe* by Aisha Ikramuddin www.checnet.org/healthehouse/education/articles-detail.asp?Main_ID=442 and *Clean Carpets Without Dangerous Chemicals* by Aisha Ikramuddin www.checnet.org/healthehouse/education/top10-detail.asp?top10_cat_ID=21
c. National Geographic Green Guide article:

Are There Any Green Carpet Cleaners? By Danielle Masterson www.thegreenguide.com/doc/ask/carpetclean

(14) Air freshener ingredients
a. Look up your particular brand in the Household Products Database at www.householdproducts.nlm.nih.gov/products.htm. There, you'll find links to TOXNET and PubMed articles and resources.
b. Childrens Health Environmental Coalition (CHEC) article: *Fragrances in Air Fresheners and Deodorizers*, by Pamela Lundquist www.checnet.org/healthehouse/education/articles-detail.asp?Main_ID=512

Laundry

(15) Chlorine bleach fumes aggravate asthmatic conditions
a. The Daily Mail (dailymail.co.uk) article: *Superclean Houses Could Cause Asthma in Children*, 24 December 2004 www.dailymail.co.uk/pages/live/articles/health/womenfamily.html?in_article_id=331815&in_page_id=1799
b. Also of interest: *2004 Annual Report on Work-Related Asthma in Michigan*, compiled by the Michigan State University Dept of Medicine and the Michigan Dept of Labor and Economic Growth. www.oem.msu.edu/asthma/04AsthmaAnnRpt_all.pdf

(16) PERC banned in CA, toxicity of PERC
a. MSNBC.com/Associated Press article: *California Air Regulators Ban Dry Cleaning Chemical.* Updated 25 Jan 2007. www.msnbc.msn.com/id/16816627

b. CBSNews.com article, *Cancer Danger from Dry Cleaning?* 23 Feb 2007
www.cbsnews.com/stories/2007/02/23/earlyshow/contributors/tracysmith/main2507444.shtml
c. The Environmental Defense Council (Canada) Toxic Nation Glossary:
www.environmentaldefence.ca/toxicnation/resources/glossary.htm

Non-Toxic Nurseries

(17) formaldehyde on baby bedding
a. click on
www.naturallygood.net/articles.htm for a list of helpful articles
b. Natural Geographic's Green Guide article: *Baby's Natural Nursery*, by Kathy Gibbons, Ph.D., and Mindy Pennybacker.
www.thegreenguide.com/doc/28/nursery
c. Environmental Illness Resource Article (ei-resource.org): *Toxic Sleep*, by Dr. Theresa Warner.
www.ei-resource.org/Articles/mcs/mcs-art22.asp
d. Also, many organic bedding retailers have information in their stores and on their websites

(18) Dangers of PVC
a. Greenpeace has many articles devoted to the dangers of PVC: see
www.greenpeace.org
b. Ecocycle.org article: *Dangers of PVC (#3) Plastics* (archived)
www.ecocycle.org/askeco-cycle/2005/0318.cfm
c. www.pvcinformation.org
d. Making Our Milk Safe (MOMS) web page

has links www.safemilk.org
e. Center for Health, Environment and Justice www.pvcfree.org
f. Article: *Polyvinyl Chloride (PVC) and the Breasts of Mothers*, by Sandra Steingraber
www.whale.to/w/polyvinyl_chloride_breastmilk.htm

(19) VOC's found in paints, turpentine, others
a. The Green Home Guide (greenhomeguide.com) article: *The Trouble with Latex: Why Common Paints Can Be Harmful, and What You Can Do About It,* by Al Hodgson, 30 Aug 2005
www.greenhomeguide.com/index.php/knowhow /entry/776/C224/
b. Sustainable Build (sustainablebuild.co.uk) article: *Non-toxic Paints*
www.sustainablebuild.co.uk/NonToxicPaint.html
(20) Carpet out-gassing and fumes
a. Green Guide Product Report: Carpets
www.thegreenguide.com/reports/product.mhtml?id=35
b. New York Times Article: *Dupont Denies Poisoning Consumers with Teflon Products*, by Amy Cortese. 8 Aug, 2004
www.organicconsumers.org/foodsafety/teflon080904.cfm

(21) Vinyl flooring emissions
a. Greenpeace articles, *PVC: the Poison Plastic*
www.greenpeace.org/international/campaigns/toxics/polyvinyl-chloride/the-poison-plastic
and *How to Find and Avoid Toxic Vinyl (PVC) in Your Home*
www.greenpeace.org/usa/news/how-to-find-and-avoid-toxic-vi
b. Asthma Regional Council article: *Health*

Considerations in Choosing School Flooring, by Francis Gilmore, MS, CIH www.asthmaregionalcouncil.org/documents/ Flooringfactsheetfinal.doc
c. Building Green (buildinggreen.com) article: *Should We Phase Out PVC?* By Nadav Malin and Alex Wilson, from Environmental Building News Jan/Feb 1994 www.buildinggreen.com/auth/article.cfm?file Name=030101b.xml

(22) SIDS may be linked to toxic baby bedding
a. HealthyChild.com. Articles: *Has the Cause of Crib Death (SIDS) Been Found?* www.healthychild.com/SIDS-crib-death-cause. htm; and *Crib Death (SIDS) from Toxic Gases in Mattresses: Factors that May Increase the Risk*, www.healthychild.com/SIDS-crib-death-factors.htm. Both articles include a complete list of references.
b. Book: The Cot Death Cover-Up? Jim Sprott, (Penguin Books New Zealand 1996). This book presents an interesting theory about the link between PVC and bedding treatments and crib death. Read an excerpt at www.cotlife2000.com/ (click on link in the left sidebar)
c. Midwifery Today article: *Baby's Bedding: Is It Creating Toxic Nerve Gasses?* By Joanne B. Quinn, RMA, PhD. First published in Midwifery Today Issue 61, Spring 2002. www.midwiferytoday.com/articles/bedding. asp?a=1&r=1&e=1&q=sids+crib+mattress
d. Also check out the FAQ Page from The Natural Sleep Store at www.thenaturalsleepstore.com/whybuyorganic faq.html

and the numerous links and articles at www.cotlife2000.com/ - especially Mattress-Wrapping Statistics and Research.

Please note: There have been studies conducted which both refute and support the theories presented the articles recommended: you'll find links to many of them on the web pages listed above.

(23) Stain-resistant treatments
a. New York Times Article: *Dupont Denies Poisoning Consumers with Teflon Products,* by Amy Cortese. 8 Aug, 2004 www.organicconsumers.org/foodsafety/ teflon080904.cfm
b. Pollution in People (pollutioninpeople.com) article: *Perfluorinated Compounds (PFC's): Stain Protector Leave an Indelible Mark*, www.pollutioninpeople.org/toxics/pfcs
c. Detoxifynow.com article, Toxin Buildup is Highest in Young, by Paul Brown, 8 Oct, 2004 www.detoxifynow.com/toxin_children. html

Back to Basics

(24) Vinegar has antibacterial, antimicrobial properties
a. Journal of Food Protection Article: *Antibacterial Action of Vinegar Against Food-Borne Pathogenic Bacteria Including Escherichia Coli.* By E. Entani; M. Asai; S. Tsujihata; Y. Tsukamoto; M. Ohta. Published August 1998, v.61(8), Pages 953-959. Find on PubMed or follow this link: www.grande.nal.usda.gov/ibids/index. php?mode2=detail&origin=ibids_

notes

credits, acknowledgements, & other heartfelt thanks

My sincere thanks to Marianna Zotos for layout and graphic organization of this book.

A great big thanks to Sara and Jack McConnell for letting us take over their beautiful kitchen for a day to shoot the back cover photo!

Also, many thanks to photographer Cassandra Birocco for all her wonderful work, including the back cover photograph, and many of the beautiful photos on our web site.

Much of the photography in this book comes from the generous contributors of the stock.xchng community. Thanks in particular to the following artists:

Jason Boutsayaphat, p. 2
Marja Flick-Buijs, p. 4
Samuel Rosa, p. 6

Valerie C. Fouche, p. 8
Louise Docker, p.9
　　　　www.sxc.hu/gallery/ladyaustin
Pat Herman, p. 10
Fleur Suijten, p. 12
Niels Timmer, Netherlands, p.13
Francois Carstens, p. 14
Mauricio W. Smith, p. 16
Marlon Paul Bruin, p. 18
　　　　kaleidoscope-king.blogspot.com
Davide Guglielmo, p. 21
Jean Scheijen, 22
Lukasz Brzozowski, p. 24
Richard Sweet, p. 26
　　　　www.richardsweet.com
Daniel Wildman, p. 28
　　　　www.sxc.hu/gallery/danzo08
Cécile Graat, p. 32
Susann Cavokaz, p. 34
Gavin Mills, p. 36
Lyn Belisle, p. 40
Meliha Gojak, p. 42
Victoria Shepherd, p. 44

afterword

Hopefully, I've given you the tools you need to start Cleaning Your Home Healthy. But you don't have to go it alone: I'm here to help!

Just go to www.yourlifeorganized.com: You can email me with questions and suggestions, catch up on the latest Your Life Organized news, even schedule a personal consultation with me. Also, please visit www.yourlifeorganized.typepad.com, my personal blog, for articles on all manner of organizing subjects.

I truly appreciate your purchase of this book, and I hope that you'll return to Your Life Organized for all your home organizing and green cleaning needs.

Cheers!
Candita Clayton

about the authors

Candita Clayton is a professional home organizer, author, and consultant. Since founding **Your Life Organized** in 2001, she has helped hundreds of people improve their daily lives using the power of home organization. Prior to launching her current career, Candita worked as a personal fitness consultant and nutritionist for seventeen years. She currently resides in the Providence, RI area with her husband and two children.

Bryna René is a freelance writer based in Warren, RI. She is the author of several short stories, and is currently hard at work on the next **Your Life Organized** publication.

BONUS

A special gift for Clean Your Home Healthy readers!

Here's what you'll get:

Free articles

Updated resources with the latest news and green trends

Inclusion in my online green makeover contests

To receive your bonus material visit me at www.yourlifeorganized.typepad.com

Also don't forget to visit us at www.yourlifeorganized.com for information on the latest products and services.

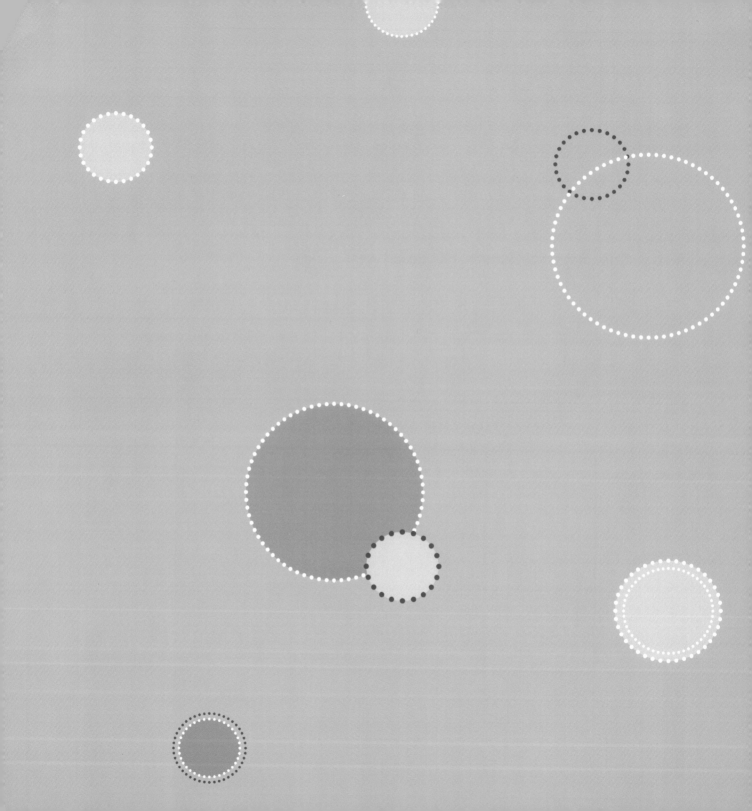

Printed in the United States
106778LV00002BA